1000

facts about

SPACE

PAM BEASANT

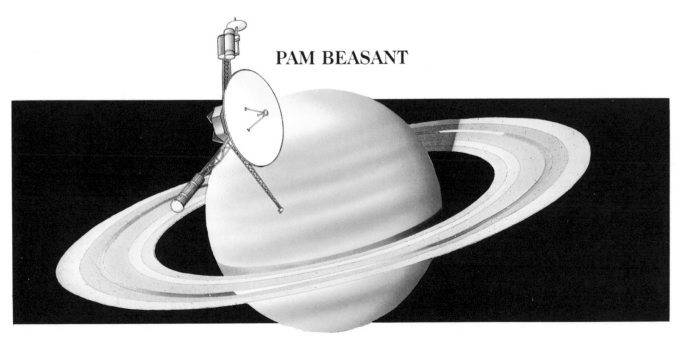

SCHOLASTIC INC.
New York Toronto London Auckland Sydney

Contents

ISBN 0-590-48681-0

Copyright © 1992 by Times Four Publishing Ltd. All rights reserved. Published by Scholastic Inc., 555 Broadway, New York, NY 10012, by arrangement with Larousse Kingfisher Chambers, Inc.

12 11 10 9 8 7 6 5 4 3   5 6 7 8 9/9 0/0

Printed in the U.S.A.   14

First Scholastic printing, February 1995

Introduction

In this book you can find out many fascinating facts about space. You can read about our own planet, Earth, and our own star, the Sun, as well as all the other planets and smaller space bodies that orbit around the Sun. You can also read about the galaxy to which our star belongs, and find out something about the millions of other galaxies that exist.

Find out, too, how space travel developed, and how rockets, satellites, and probes have helped scientists to discover so much more about the mysteries of the universe.

Also, there are lots of easy-to-find facts beginning with a spot, like this:

● The Moon is moving slowly away from Earth at a rate of an inch (3 cm) per year.

Across the top of each page there is a list of useful mini-facts — for example, the distance of planets from the Sun, or the kinds of space telescopes in orbit.

On each double page there is a Strange but True section containing some unusual or startling facts.

On pages 42–45 you will find charts and lists of space records and facts for you to refer to.

If you are not sure where to find out about a particular topic, look in the Index on pages 46–48.

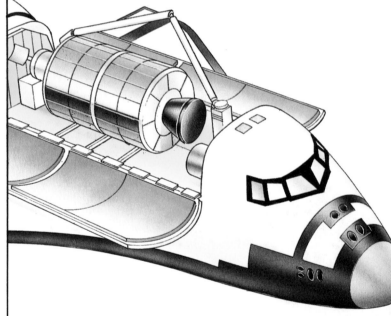

To help you pick out the things you want to read about, some key words are in bold type like this: **planets**.

The Universe

The universe goes on for ever. Most of it is **empty space**, with huge swarms of stars called **galaxies** shining out into the blackness. Our Sun belongs to a galaxy called the **Milky Way** containing about 100 billion stars. There are billions of galaxies in the universe.

The Solar System

The **Solar System** is the name given to our Sun and all the space bodies that revolve around it, including the Earth.

● There are nine planets and over 60 moons, or satellites, all spinning as they orbit or travel around the Sun.

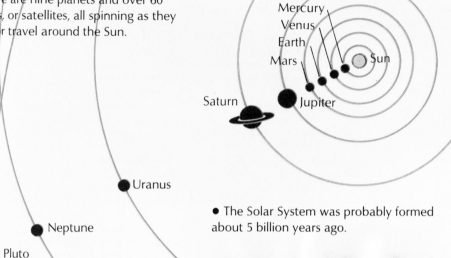

Mercury
Venus
Earth
Mars
Sun
Saturn
Jupiter
Uranus
Neptune
Pluto

● The Solar System was probably formed about 5 billion years ago.

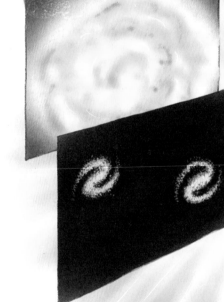

The Big Bang theory

Most scientists believe the universe began about 14 billion years ago with a gigantic explosion they call the **Big Bang**.

● The bang blasted hot material out in all directions. It was far hotter than a nuclear explosion, or even the center of the Sun.

● As this material cooled, it turned into hydrogen and helium. These are the two most common "elements," or substances, found in the universe.

● Galaxies and stars began to form out of hydrogen and helium about a billion years after the Big Bang.

Our Sun is a star. Other stars may also have planets, comets, and other space bodies circling around them. There are probably other planets like the Earth in the universe.

Clues to the Big Bang

There are some **clues** to show that the Big Bang happened. Two of the most important clues are:

● The galaxies are flying farther apart, as if from the force of an explosion.

● Space is still slightly "warm" from the last traces of the explosion.

Theories about the future

There are **two main theories** about what will happen to the universe in the future. They are:

- The Open Theory, which says that the universe started with the Big Bang and the galaxies will carry on expanding for ever.

- The Closed Theory, which says that the universe will stop expanding. The pulling force of gravity will slowly drag the galaxies back toward each other again until there is a Big Crunch!

- The latest observations made by astronomers show that the Open Theory is more likely to be the correct one.

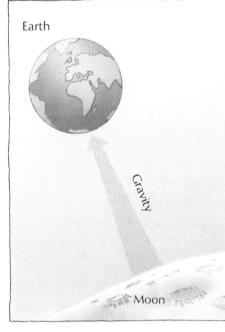

Earth

Gravity

Moon

Gravity

Gravity is the **pulling force** that exists between things. It is the force that keeps the Moon revolving around the Earth.

- The Sun's gravity keeps the planets in orbit, and stops them from flying off into space as they spin around.

- The Sun has a much greater pull of gravity than the Earth, because it has 333,000 times as much mass (amount of material) as Earth.

- Your weight is the force of the Earth's gravity pulling you down onto its surface.

Measuring Space

Distances in space are too vast to be measured in miles, so scientists measure in **light-years**. A light-year is 5.88 trillion miles (9.46 trillion km) — the distance traveled by light in one year.

- The nearest star to the Sun is called Proxima Centauri. It is 4.3 light-years away, which means it takes 4.3 years for its light to reach Earth.

Hubble space telescope (see p.31)

Strange but true

- The temperature when the Big Bang happened was about 1 billion billion billion °C.

- A hundredth of a second later (the time needed to take a snapshot), it had cooled to 1 billion °C.

- Most of the material in the universe is invisible. Some of it may exist as dark particles between galaxies.

Radio telescope

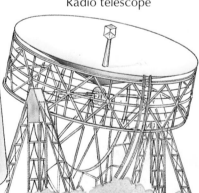

How far can we see?

- Radio telescopes on Earth have helped astronomers to detect very distant objects. The most distant galaxy so far observed by astronomers is at least 6 billion light-years away.

- Some telescopes have been put into Space. They can "see" more clearly than telescopes on Earth and can detect invisible energy waves (see p.7). One day they may discover new stars and planets.

5

The stars

The stars in the sky look small because they are so far away. In fact they are huge. Each star is a glowing **ball of gases** held together by gravity. Most of this gas is **hydrogen**. In the hot fury of a star's "core" or center, hydrogen reaches a temperature of at least 18 million°F (10 million°C).

Every element consists of tiny atoms. The heat inside a star changes hydrogen atoms into the atoms of another gas called **helium**.

When this happens there is an **"atomic reaction"** and a flash of energy is given out. Billions of these flashes of energy keep the star hot and make it shine.

The **Sun** is the nearest star to Earth. It is only a middle-sized star but it looks big to us because it is so close — only 93 million miles (150 million km) away!

The birth and death of a star

Stars are born in clusters. A **cloud of gas and dust** called a **nebula** breaks up over millions of years into smaller clouds which are then pulled tighter and smaller by their own gravity. Eventually they heat up and start to shine.

A star being formed from gas and dust.

Gravity → Core ← Gravity

● After billions of years, stars finally run out of energy and die.

Supernova

Red giant

● The remains of a very large star may collapse to form a black hole.

● Larger stars do not last as long as smaller ones. They die dramatically in an explosion. The exploding star is called a supernova.

● As a star grows old, its core becomes hotter and swells up. This swollen star is called a red giant.

Black hole

Pulsar

White dwarf

● A black hole is invisible because light cannot escape from it.

● A very small, extremely dense body is left, called a neutron star.

● Some neutron stars, called pulsars, give off pulses of light and radio waves as they spin.

● Eventually the star collapses and becomes a white dwarf — a small but very hot star. It cools and finally fades away.

The electromagnetic spectrum

Stars give off different kinds of **energy waves**, or **radiation**. Each kind has a different wavelength. Together they are called the **electromagnetic spectrum**.

● We can see one kind of energy wave — visible light. The others are invisible.

● Special instruments are used to detect radiation. Dangerous X rays and gamma rays are blocked by the Earth's atmosphere and have to be studied from space.

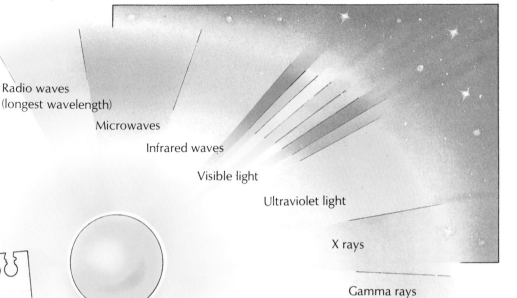

Radio waves (longest wavelength)

Microwaves

Infrared waves

Visible light

Ultraviolet light

X rays

Gamma rays (shortest wavelength)

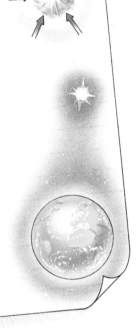

Strange but true

● Every star would explode if gravity did not hold its material together.

● When you look at the sky at night, you are also looking back in time. The light from stars takes so long to reach Earth that what you see is how the stars looked when their light began its journey to Earth centuries ago.

The Sun as a star

Sun

The Sun was formed from a **nebula** about 5 billion years ago, and will burn for about another 5 billion years.

● The Sun is the source of life on Earth. Without its light and heat, Earth would be dead and icy. (You can find out more about the Sun on pages 14–15.)

Different kinds of stars

Some stars, like the Sun, shine with a **steady light**. Other kinds of stars don't shine steadily. They are called **variable stars**.

● Some stars have a regular cycle of fading and getting brighter. For example, the star called Delta Cephei reaches full brightness every 5 days 9 hours.

● Some variable stars are really binary systems — two steadily shining stars orbiting each other. They seem to fade when one blocks light from the other and brighten when they are both visible at the same time.

● Sometimes a binary system star blazes very brightly for just a few nights. This is called a nova. It probably happens when a cloud of gas from one star explodes as it reaches the other star.

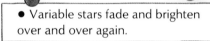

● Variable stars fade and brighten over and over again.

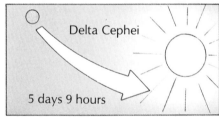

Delta Cephei

5 days 9 hours

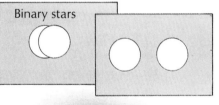

Binary stars

Nova

The constellations

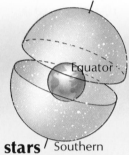

Constellations are **patterns of stars** in the night sky. The shapes they seem to make were given names in ancient times, and many of these names are still used today.

The stars that make up constellations are not really close to each other. Sometimes the stars that look closest are really far apart — they just happen to form a pattern and so look like a group when viewed from Earth.

Hemispheres

On maps, Earth is divided in half by an imaginary line called the **equator**. One half is known as the **Northern Hemisphere**. The other is called the **Southern Hemisphere**.

Some Northern Hemisphere stars

• The constellation Taurus (the Bull) contains a group of stars called the Pleiades, or the Seven Sisters (although there are actually far more than seven stars). They are 400 light-years away.

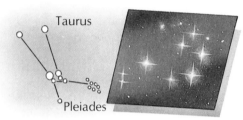

Taurus

Pleiades

• The Andromeda Galaxy (see p.11) is a dim smudge in the Andromeda constellation. It is 2 million light-years away.

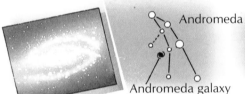

Andromeda

Andromeda galaxy

• Viewed from the Earth, stars appear to form patterns on the inside of a huge imaginary sphere. Like the Earth, this "star sphere" is also divided into Northern and Southern Hemispheres.

Northern Hemisphere

Equator

Southern Hemisphere

• The constellation Ursa Major (the Great Bear) is often called the Big Dipper. It contains a group of seven bright stars.

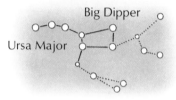

Big Dipper

Ursa Major

• Polaris, the North Star, is in the constellation Ursa Minor (the Little Bear). It appears to be fixed in the sky, and so for centuries has helped travelers find north.

Polaris

Ursa Minor

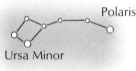
Star trails on photographic film

Star drift

During the night, stars seem to **rise**, **move** across the sky and then **sink** out of sight. They do not really move, however. It is the **turning Earth** that makes the stars appear to move across the sky.

• Stars seen from the North and South Poles appear to move around the sky in level paths, without ever rising or setting at all.

• If photographic film is exposed to a starry sky for some hours, the stars leave trails on the film as they appear to move across the sky.

Canopus	Alpha Centauri	Arcturus	Vega
magnitude minus 0.7	magnitude minus 0.3	magnitude 0.06	magnitude 0.04
230 light-years away	4.3 light-years away	38 light-years away	27 light-years away

Some Southern Hemisphere stars

● Proxima Centauri, our nearest star apart from the Sun, is part of the Centaurus constellation. It is 4.3 light-years away.

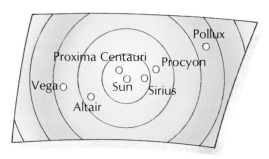

● The constellation called Canis Major (the Great Dog) contains Sirius, the brightest star in the sky. It is also called the Dog Star.

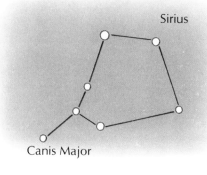

Canis Major

Sirius

● The Southern Cross is the smallest constellation. Two of its stars can be lined up to point due south, which is useful for navigation.

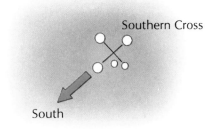

Southern Cross

South

● The Magellanic Clouds, two small irregular galaxies, are the Milky Way's closest companions in Space. They are about 200,000 light-years away.

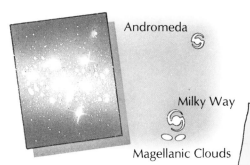

Andromeda

Milky Way

Magellanic Clouds

Orion the hunter

Some constellations, such as **Orion**, belong to both the **Northern** and the **Southern Hemispheres**.

● Orion was named after a famous hunter in ancient Greek mythology.

● Betelgeuse is a variable red giant star (see pp.6–7), in Orion.

Orion

● Three stars make up Orion's belt.

● The Horsehead Nebula, south of Orion, is a dark cloud of cold gas and dust shaped like a horse's head.

Star brightness

The brightness of a star is called its **magnitude**. Astronomers have given each star a **magnitude rating**.

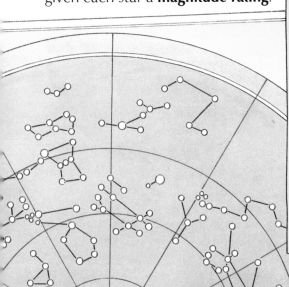

● The higher the number, the dimmer the star. The dimmest stars visible without a telescope have a magnitude of about 6. A magnitude 0 star is very bright. The brightest stars have minus numbers.

● Sirius, the brightest star in the sky, has a magnitude of minus 1.5.

Strange but true

● The African Dogon tribe say their ancestors knew about the invisible star Sirius B thousands of years before scientists discovered it in 1862.

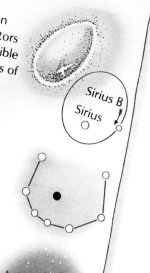

Sirius B
Sirius

● In the constellation Corona Borealis there is a star that sometimes turns very dim, almost overnight, when clouds of tiny black particles hide it from view.

● North American Indians tested warriors' eyesight by seeing how many stars of the Pleiades they could spot!

Galaxies

Galaxies are **huge groups** containing hundreds of millions of **stars**. They were probably formed about a billion years after the Big Bang (see p.4) when the universe was quite young.

No one knows how many galaxies there are in all, but there are probably billions.
 Galaxies often move together in groups, called **clusters**. Our galaxy is in a cluster of about twenty galaxies, but there are much bigger groups containing thousands of galaxies.

The Milky Way

Our galaxy is called the **Milky Way**. It contains about 100 billion stars. The **Sun** and the **Solar System** are more than halfway out from the center to the edge of the galaxy.

- It takes light about 100,000 years to travel from one side of the Milky Way to the other. (Light takes only $8\frac{1}{2}$ minutes to travel to Earth from the Sun.)

- The whole Milky Way rotates in space. It takes the Sun 225 million years to revolve once around the center of the galaxy. This is called a galactic year.

- The center of our galaxy cannot be seen from Earth because it is hidden by dust and gas.

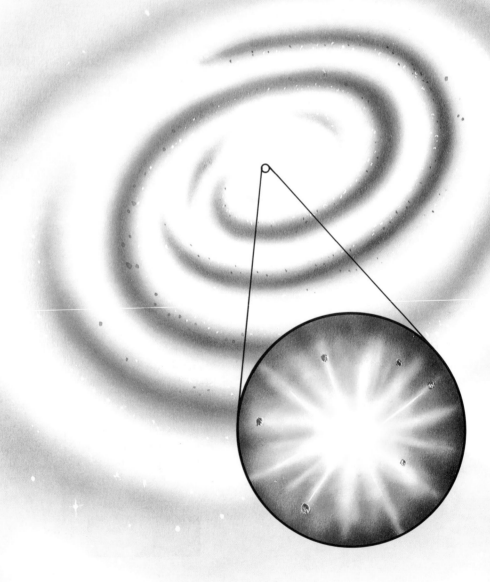

- The central bulge of the Milky Way contains almost half of all the stars in the galaxy. They are much closer together than the Sun and its neighboring stars.

- Although they are so close together in space terms, stars collide with each other in the center of the galaxy only rarely — perhaps one collision every 1,000 years.

10

Galaxy shapes

These are the four main **galaxy shapes**:

Spiral

Barred spiral

- Spirals turn like a lit pinwheel, or cream swirling in a cup of coffee. Our galaxy is a spiral.

- Barred spirals look like two tadpoles joined at the head. They have a bar shape in the center and two long arms.

Elliptical

Irregular

- Elliptical (oval) galaxies look like squashed circles. It is thought they contain older stars.

- Irregular galaxies contain a lot of dust and form no definite shape.

Strange but true

- There may be a huge black hole at the center of our galaxy that is gradually sucking in the surrounding light and gas.

- The ancient Greeks called our galaxy the Milky Way because they thought it was made from drops of milk from the breasts of the Greek goddess Hera.

- Giant elliptical (oval) galaxies, found at the center of large clusters, may be "eating up" smaller galaxies.

Neighboring galaxies

The **biggest galaxy** in our group is the **Andromeda Spiral**. It is about 2 million light-years away from Earth and contains about 400 billion stars.

- Andromeda can be seen from Earth with the naked eye.

- Our nearest galaxy neighbors are the Magellanic Clouds. These are two small irregular galaxies. The larger galaxy contains about 10 billion stars and is 180,000 light-years away. The other galaxy is much smaller and farther away.

- The Magellanic Clouds were first sighted in 1521 by the explorer, Ferdinand Magellan.

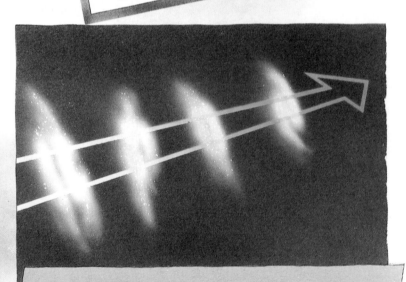

Red shift

As galaxies speed away from Earth, the light from them gets distorted so that it appears red. This is known as **red shift**. The faster a galaxy is moving away, the more red it will seem to be. The red color cannot be seen by the eye. Astronomers study it using special instruments.

Space oddities

Although scientists know much about the universe, there are still many strange things in Space that have not been fully explained. **Black holes** are the most mysterious. It seems that they exist, but they can never by seen!

Anything that falls into a black hole can never come out again because gravity will crush it to nothing.

Quasars and **cosmic rays** are other space objects that still baffle scientists. If you think of the universe as a giant jigsaw, only a few pieces have so far been fitted together.

Black holes

Some **very rare stars** contain as much material as fifty or more Suns. They are the brightest stars in the universe, yet they turn into **black holes** — the blackest objects in Space.

1. When these stars die (see p.6) they keep on shrinking, because the pull of gravity is so strong.

2. They shrink down to a tiny speck, called a singularity or a black hole.

3. Although tiny, the black hole contains all the material from the huge star.

4. A black hole's gravity is so strong that no light can escape from it.

5. Astronomers have not seen a black hole, but they have found stars they think may have a black hole nearby.

Quasars

Quasars are very distant objects that send out far more **light** than ordinary galaxies. They may also send out strong **radio waves**.

● Quasars seem to be sending out tremendous energy from a small space inside them. This could come from gas whirling around a giant black hole at the center of the galaxy.

● The name "quasar" is short for quasi-stellar (starlike) object.

● Quasars may have been a stage that some galaxies went through early in their lives. Because they are billions of light-years away, we are seeing them today as they were billions of years ago.

Detecting black holes

Some **binary star systems** (see p.7) may contain a star that has turned into a **black hole**. Gas from the other star would swirl around the black hole before being pulled into it, giving off high-energy radiation, including X rays.

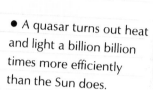
Earth

- X rays cannot travel through Earth's atmosphere, so they are studied by satellites that send information back to Earth.

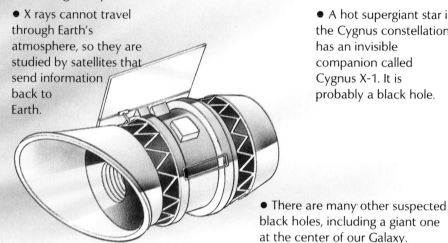

- A hot supergiant star in the Cygnus constellation has an invisible companion called Cygnus X-1. It is probably a black hole.

- There are many other suspected black holes, including a giant one at the center of our Galaxy.

Strange but true

- If the Sun became a black hole, it would be only a few miles across — but it could swallow the Earth!

- A quasar turns out heat and light a billion billion times more efficiently than the Sun does.

- Cosmic rays can affect tree growth. Some astronomers have studied tree rings to find out how the number of cosmic rays reaching the Earth has changed over the centuries.

Cosmic rays and neutrinos

Cosmic rays are tiny **particles** that travel in space at high speed and constantly shower Earth. They may come from exploding **stars**. Most of them do not penetrate Earth's atmosphere.

- Some cosmic rays bounce off into space

Earth's atmosphere

- Some cosmic rays reach the Earth's surface.

Exploding star

Cosmic rays

- Some cosmic ray particles are called neutrinos. These can pass right through the Earth itself as if it were not there!

- Several million neutrinos will pass through you as you read this page!

Neutrinos pass right through the Earth.

New planets?

There are nine planets in our Solar System. Scientists are trying to find **other planets** circling other stars.

- Throughout the universe, there are probably millions of other stars with solar systems. Each could have its own planets.

- So far, no other planets have been found for certain. Radio astronomers who thought they had found a planet outside the Solar System in 1991 later announced that they had made a computer error.

The Sun

The Sun, like all stars, is a ball of fiercely **hot gas**. Hydrogen gas deep inside it is constantly being turned into helium (see p.6). This releases energy in the form of **light** and **heat**.

The Sun is the nearest star to Earth. In space terms it is relatively close — only about 93 million miles (150 million km) away!

The Sun has shone steadily for thousands of millions of years. If it went dim for only a few days, most life-forms on Earth would perish.

Features of the Sun

These are some of the Sun's more **spectacular features**:

● Enormous eruptions of gas, called prominences, rise continually from the surface of the Sun. Some reach out into Space as far as 1.2 million miles (2 million km).

Arched prominences

Sunspots

● Sunspots are darker, cooler areas that appear on the Sun's surface from time to time. Some are much larger than the Earth and can last for months. Smaller ones last for only a few days or weeks.

● Every 11 years or so, sunspots become more common and then fade away. This is called the sunspot cycle.

Solar flares

● Solar flares are violent explosions of energy from the Sun's surface. They shoot particles at high speed out into space. On Earth they can produce strange effects, such as the glowing lights, called aurorae, that sometimes appear in the night sky.

Sun facts

● The diameter of the Sun is 865,000 miles (1,392,000 km)

● The temperature at the core is believed to be about 25 million °F (14 million °C). At the surface it is 11,000°F (6,000°C).

● A million bodies the size of the Earth could be squashed inside the Sun.

● The Sun is 92 percent hydrogen. At the center is a core of helium. Around this core 4 million tons of the Sun's material is turned into energy every second.

Different parts of the Sun rotate at different speeds.

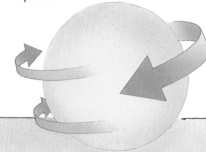

Different speeds

● Because the Sun is made of gases, different parts of it can rotate at different speeds. The center part, or equator area, rotates faster than the poles.

● Energy from the core takes a million years to reach the Sun's surface, but only $8\frac{1}{2}$ minutes to travel from the Sun's surface to the Earth.

Chromosphere — a layer a few thousand miles deep that shines pink during an eclipse

Corona — the outer atmosphere that stretches millions of miles into space

WARNING Never look directly at the Sun. It can damage your eyes and blind you.

Solar eclipses

Occasionally the **Moon** passes in front of the Sun so that it **blocks out sunlight** from part of the Earth. This is called a **total solar eclipse**.

● If the eclipse is total, the Sun's faint atmosphere or corona shines out in the darkened sky. This is the only time it can be seen from Earth.

● During a total eclipse, prominences can sometimes be seen flaring out around the darkened outline of the Sun. Eclipses provide scientists with good opportunities for studying such things as prominences and the corona.

● When the Moon blocks out only part of the Sun's light, this is called a partial eclipse.

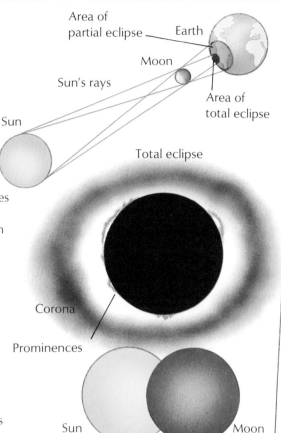

Area of partial eclipse

Earth

Moon

Sun's rays

Sun

Area of total eclipse

Total eclipse

Corona

Prominences

Sun

Moon

Partial eclipse

Strange but true

● The Sun is described by scientists as a yellow dwarf star.

● There may be a connection between the appearance of sunspots and changes in the weather on Earth.

● Sound waves produced inside the Sun make it swell and shrink by a mile or so every few minutes.

What will happen to the Sun?

Like all stars, the Sun is **changing**. This is what scientists believe will happen to it:

1. Several billion years from now, the Sun will have a crisis. The hydrogen supply around its core will start to run out, and our star will begin to collapse.

2. This collapse will put new energy into the core so the Sun will blaze hotter than ever.

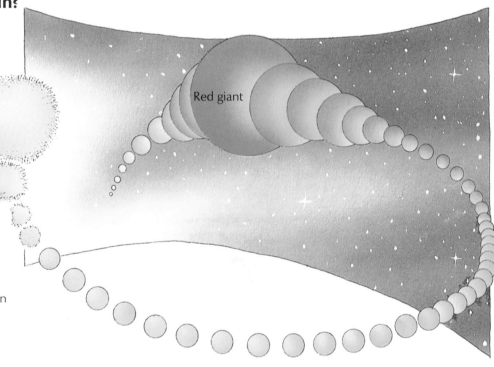

Red giant

3. The blast of energy will force the higher gas layers outward. The Sun will become a red giant, 100 times its present diameter and 500 times brighter.

4. The red giant will fill Earth's sky. The great heat will melt the surface of the Earth into seas of lava.

5. Eventually the Sun will cool and shrink, becoming a white dwarf star (see p.6) about the size of Earth.

The Moon

The Moon is an airless ball of **rock** about a quarter the diameter of the Earth. It circles around the Earth once every 27.3 days. It has no **light** of its own, but reflects light from the Sun.

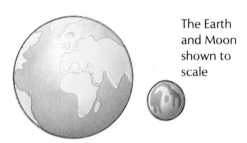

The Earth and Moon shown to scale

The Moon has probably always been lifeless, but it has had a violent, turbulent history. Most of the **craters** on its surface were caused by solid space bodies called meteoroids crashing into it between 3 and 4 billion years ago. The darker areas are called **maria** (seas). They are made of lava that flowed out from inside the Moon about 3 billion years ago.

Gravity

The Moon is much smaller than Earth and so has much weaker **gravity**. Astronauts had to be weighted down to help them walk properly on the Moon's surface.

Astronauts on the Moon

Phases of the Moon

The Moon keeps the same **side** facing Earth all the time, so we only see this one side of it. As the Moon travels around the Earth, we see a varying amount of this side each day, depending on how much of it is sunlit. These different amounts, or stages, are called the **phases of the Moon**.

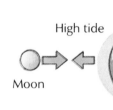
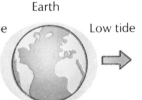

● It is gravity that causes ocean tides on Earth to rise and fall. The gravity of the Sun and Moon pulls the Earth's oceans into bulges. The Earth rotates beneath these bulges, producing two high tides a day.

Earth

High tide   Low tide   Sun

Moon

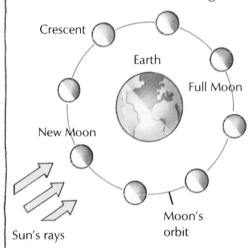

Crescent

Earth

Full Moon

New Moon

Sun's rays

Moon's orbit

● When the Moon is seen as a crescent, only a sliver of the side facing Earth is sunlit.

● As the Moon moves around the Earth, it appears half-lit and then finally fully lit (the Full Moon). At this stage the whole of the side facing Earth is sunlit.

● After Full Moon, the shape changes back to half and finally to a thin crescent. It then disappears for a few nights (New Moon) and the process begins again.

● It takes 29.5 days for the Moon to move through all its phases from New, through Full, and back to New again.

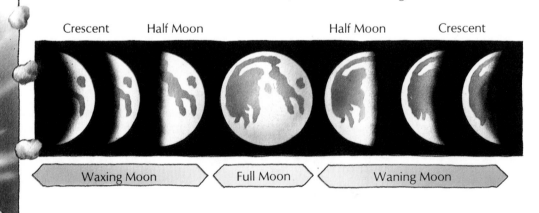

Crescent   Half Moon   Half Moon   Crescent

Waxing Moon   Full Moon   Waning Moon

● As the Moon grows from crescent to Full, it is called the waxing moon.

● As it shrinks back to a crescent, it is called the waning moon.

The Moon's surface

The Moon's **surface** is covered with craters, ridges, mountains, and valleys. The dark maria are the smoothest parts because the lava that created them flowed over and covered old craters. These are some facts about the Moon's surface:

● The biggest Moon crater that can be seen from Earth is called Bailly. It is about 180 miles (290 km) across.

● The largest Moon crater is on the far side of the Moon and so cannot be seen from Earth.

● Because the Moon has no air or water to wear rocks away, the Moon's surface has remained unchanged for thousands of millions of years.

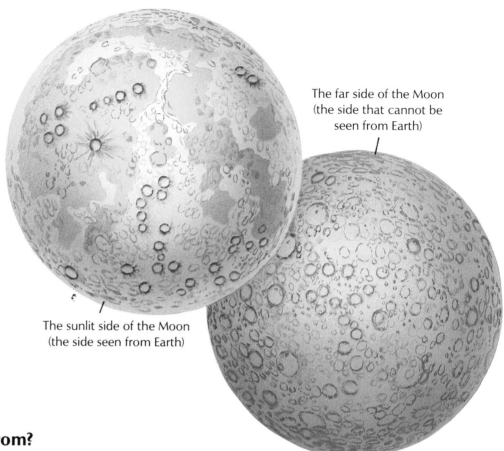

The far side of the Moon (the side that cannot be seen from Earth)

The sunlit side of the Moon (the side seen from Earth)

Where did the Moon come from?

The Moon and Earth are roughly the same age. Scientists are unsure where the Moon came from. Here are four theories:

1. The Moon and Earth formed together from the same dust and gas cloud.

2. The Moon was a wandering space body that came close to Earth and became trapped in Earth's orbit.

3. When the Earth was young and molten, it grew a bulge that spun off and became the Moon.

4. A small planet hit the young molten Earth and threw material into orbit, which got drawn together to form the Moon.

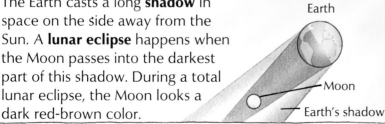

Strange but true

● The Moon is moving slowly away from Earth at the rate of an inch per year.

● The far side of the Moon was not seen until 1959 when the Soviet spacecraft Luna 3 flew by and took pictures of it.

● Earth's gravity has pulled on the side of the Moon that faces Earth, causing a bulge several miles high.

● It would take 81 Moons to weigh the same as Earth.

Lunar eclipses

The Earth casts a long **shadow** in space on the side away from the Sun. A **lunar eclipse** happens when the Moon passes into the darkest part of this shadow. During a total lunar eclipse, the Moon looks a dark red-brown color.

Sun

Earth

Moon

Earth's shadow

Earth and the Solar System

Earth is a smallish, rocky planet. It is in just the right place in the Solar System to allow **life** to be supported. If Earth were nearer to the Sun, it would be too hot for life as we know it to survive. If it were farther away, it would be too cold.

Seen from Space, Earth is a beautiful **bluish disk** with swirling white clouds. It looks blue because so much of its surface is ocean.

Earth seen from space

Earth's position in the Solar System

Earth is the third planet from the Sun. Its closest neighbors are Venus and Mars.

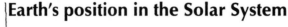

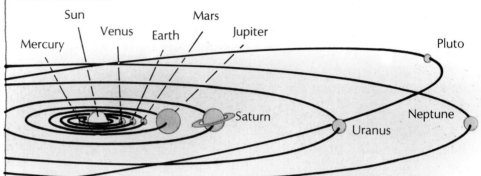

Sun · Mercury · Venus · Earth · Mars · Jupiter · Saturn · Uranus · Neptune · Pluto

How the Earth began

Earth was formed about 4.6 billion years ago, from **small rocky bodies** that collided with each other as they whirled around the Sun.

● These collisions gave out so much energy that the Earth glowed red-hot as farther rocky bodies crashed into it.

● After several hundred million years, Earth reached its present size. The collisions died down and the Earth started to cool.

● The metal in the Earth sank to the center, forming the core, with the lighter rocks forming the mantle and crust.

Crust, mantle, and core

This is what the Earth might look like inside. At the center is the **core**, surrounded by the **mantle**. The **crust** is a thin layer on the surface.

● The Earth's core is about 4,500 miles (7,000 km) across and is probably made of iron and nickel. The outer part is liquid and the inner part solid.

● The mantle is made of rock. It contains most of the Earth's material.

● The crust is made of lighter rocks that floated to the top when Earth was molten. It varies from 4 to 25 miles (6 to 40 km) thick.

Crust · Mantle · Outer core · Inner core

Strange but true

● The Icelandic island of Surtsey was formed between 1963 and 1966. It began when an underwater volcano suddenly erupted, shooting columns of lava high into the air.

● Some underwater volcanoes are higher than Mount Everest.

● The Himalayan mountains were formed when India (then an island) collided with the rest of Asia.

Earth's atmosphere

Earth is surrounded by an **atmosphere**, which enables life to survive on the planet. This is what the atmosphere does:

- Provides the air we breathe.

- Protects Earth from harmful rays from Space (see p.7).

- Protects Earth from space debris, such as meteors.

- Stops Earth getting too cold at night or too hot in the day.

Layers of the atmosphere

The atmosphere can be divided into these **different layers**:

- Exosphere (300–5,000 miles (500–8,000 km) above the Earth) Weather satellites orbit in this layer.

- Ionosphere (50–300 miles (80–500 km) above the Earth) This layer protects the Earth from harmful rays.

- Mesosphere (30–50 miles (48–80 km) above the Earth) Unmanned balloons have measured the temperature of this layer.

- Stratosphere (6–30 miles (10–48 km) above the Earth) Jet aircraft fly in this layer.

- The ozone layer is part of the stratosphere, at about 25 miles (40 km) high.

- Troposphere (From the ground to 6 miles (10 km) high) We live in this layer and all Earth's weather happens in it.

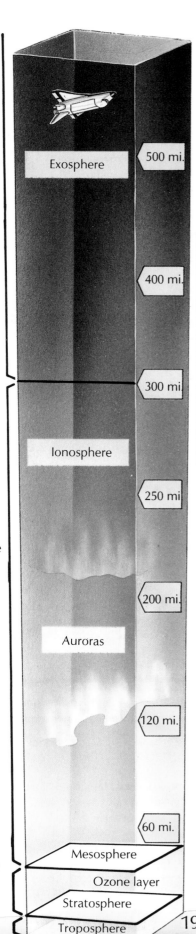

Exosphere
500 mi.
400 mi.
300 mi.
Ionosphere
250 mi
200 mi.
Auroras
120 mi.
60 mi.
Mesosphere
Ozone layer
Stratosphere
Troposphere

Volcanoes

Volcanoes are openings in the Earth's crust where melted rock from inside bursts through to the surface. Some melted rock (called **lava**) spills out. It can build up around the opening to form a **mountain**.

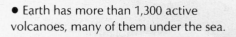

Lava

Molten rock

- Earth has more than 1,300 active volcanoes, many of them under the sea.

- The islands of Hawaii and Iceland are made of rock that erupted out of the sea from underwater volcanoes.

- Most volcanoes are found near where the plates of the Earth's crust (see below) collide with each other.

Plates

The Earth's **crust** in not an unbroken shell. It is a jigsaw of about 15 huge **rocky pieces** called **plates** that continually push and slide against each other.

- When two plates collide, the rocks they are made of can get squashed and pushed up into the air. Some mountains were formed that way.

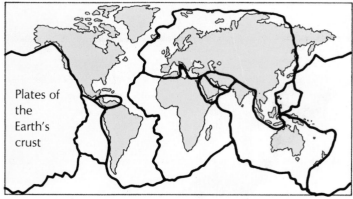

Plates of the Earth's crust

- Earthquakes are caused by the plates of the Earth's crust sliding against each other.

- The surface of the Earth is changing all the time as rocks wear down and plates move.

The nearest planets

The nearest planets to Earth are **Mercury**, **Venus**, and **Mars**. They all have a solid, **rocky surface**, like Earth's.

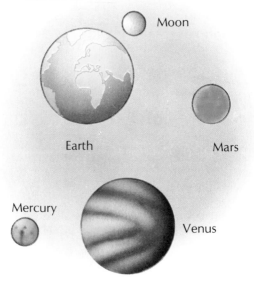

Moon

Earth

Mars

Mercury

Venus

Space probes have taken photographs of Venus, Mars, and Mercury and studied their surfaces. Some people thought there was a slight chance of finding **life** on Mars, but no sign of life was found on any of these planets.

Mercury facts

Mercury is the **closest planet** to the Sun. It has:

● Extremely hot days, with temperatures of 650°F (350°C), because it is so close to the Sun.

● Very cold nights, because there is no atmosphere to trap the daytime heat.

● An iron core, like the Earth's.

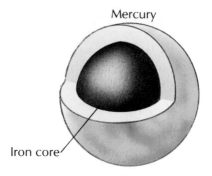

Mercury

Iron core

● Earth is $2\frac{1}{2}$ times bigger than Mercury.

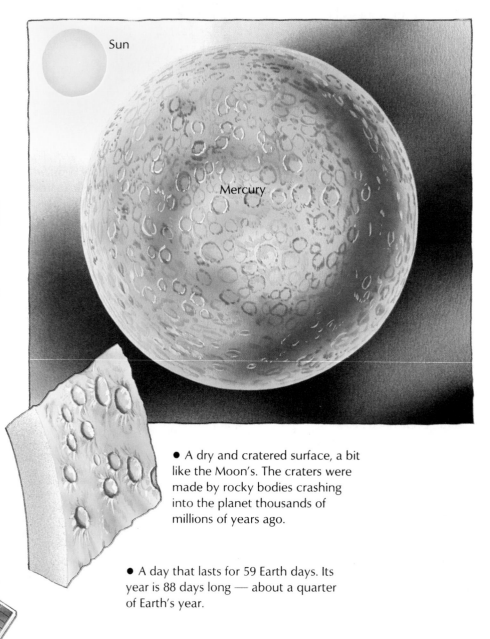

Sun

Mercury

● A dry and cratered surface, a bit like the Moon's. The craters were made by rocky bodies crashing into the planet thousands of millions of years ago.

● A day that lasts for 59 Earth days. Its year is 88 days long — about a quarter of Earth's year.

● Mercury spins around the Sun faster than any other planet. This is how it came by its name. In Ancient Greek mythology, Mercury was the swift messenger of the gods.

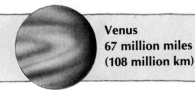
Venus
67 million miles
(108 million km)

Earth
93 million miles
(150 million km)

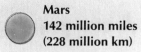
Mars
142 million miles
(228 million km)

Venus facts

Venus (named after the goddess of love) is the closest planet to Earth and shines more brightly than any other planet. It has:

● Heavy, swirling clouds that hide the mountains and craters on its surface. The clouds trap the Sun's heat, raising the temperature to around 900°F (480°C).

● Three large highland areas surrounded by deserts. These have been seen only by radar, as clouds cover them from view.

● An atmosphere of mainly unbreatheable carbon dioxide. There are constant thunderstorms, with drops of sulfuric acid in the clouds.

Venus

● Venus is similar in size to the Earth.

● Ishtar Terra, a highland area of Venus, is larger than the U.S.A.

Strange but true

● Venus's day is very long. It takes 243 days to spin once, and only 224 days to go around the Sun.

● Clouds on Venus spin around the planet in only four days.

● Mars has a volcano, called Olympus Mons, that stretches 15 miles (25 km) above the planet's surface. It is the largest volcano in the Solar System.

Mars facts

Mars is the farthest inner planet from the Sun. It looks red from Earth, which is why it was named after Mars, the god of war. Mars has:

● A barren, dusty surface with reddish soil and rocks. There are deep canyons and high volcanoes.

● A day that lasts for 24 hours, 37 minutes — almost the same as Earth's. Its year, however, is nearly twice as long as Earth's — 687 days.

● A thin atmosphere of carbon dioxide that does not block the Sun's harmful radiation. It is cold, with temperatures averaging −9°C (−23°C).

● Occasional large dust storms that are visible through a telescope from Earth.

● Spectacular white icy caps at its north and south poles. These grow and shrink depending on the Martian seasons.

● A long time ago, some astronomers thought there might be intelligent life on Mars because regular lines on the planet's surface looked as if they had been made by intelligent beings.

Mars's surface

● Mars has two very small natural satellites, or moons, called Phobos and Deimos. Phobos is 14 miles (22 km) across. Deimos is 9 miles (14 km) across.

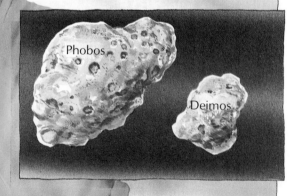

Phobos

Deimos

Asteroids, comets, and meteoroids

Asteroids are mini-planets that orbit the Sun. Most of them are less than a mile across. **Comets** are lumps of dirty ice, dust, and rock. Most of them move in long oval-shaped orbits around the Sun. **Meteoroids** are rocky fragments, varying in size from a grain of sand up to a few inches across. If they enter Earth's atmosphere they usually burn up in flashes of light known as **meteors**. However, larger meteoroids are not always destroyed and may land on Earth. Then they become known as **meteorites**.

The asteroid belt

The **asteroid belt** lies between the orbits of Mars and Jupiter. It probably contains at least 40,000 **tiny planets** over half a mile across, revolving around the Sun.

● Astronomers once thought asteroids were fragments on one mini-planet that broke up. Evidence now suggests they are fragments of smaller bodies that collided with each other.

● The asteroid belt makes journeys dangerous for spacecraft, which can be destroyed if they hit even a tiny object. Fortunately, the asteroids are several miles apart!

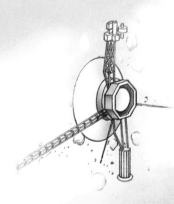

Comets

Comets are made of crumbly **rock** and **ice**. Most travel in long orbits that stretch from near the Sun to the outer part of the Solar System.

● When a comet is near the Sun, the heat turns some of the ice to gas. It streams out behind the comet's head in a glowing tail that may be tens of millions of miles long.

● Comets freeze down to a small, dark core when they are far from the Sun.

● Some comets go right around the Sun every few years. Others take thousands or even millions of years to do so because their orbits are so huge.

● Halley's Comet takes 76 years to orbit the Sun. It was last seen in 1986, although it was much less spectacular than on its previous appearance in 1910.

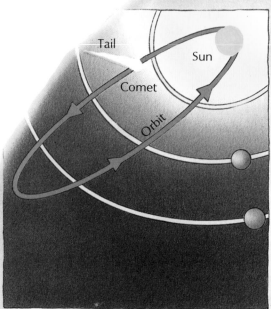

Strange but true

● Halley's Comet was seen in 1066, before the Battle of Hastings. William the Conqueror believed it was a sign that he would win the battle.

● In Greenland, people dig up meteorites and use the iron in them to make tools.

● In 1908, forests in Siberia were flattened by a strange explosion. It may have been caused by a meteorite hitting the Earth.

Meteors

Meteors are the **bright streaks** seen when **meteoroids** burn up as they hurtle through the atmosphere at up to 30 miles per second (50 km/sec). They are often called **shooting stars**.

● Shooting stars (meteors) are seen more often when the Earth travels through a swarm of meteoroids in its path around the Sun. This is known as a meteor shower. The most famous meteor shower is called the Perseids.

● More than 20 million meteoroids are thought to enter Earth's atmosphere every day. Most burn up.

Meteorites

Meteorites are large **meteoroids** that do not burn up completely in the Earth's atmosphere. They fall to the ground.

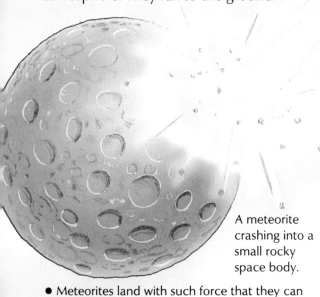

A meteorite crashing into a small rocky space body.

● Meteorites land with such force that they can make holes in the ground called craters. Craters can be seen on many planets and their satellites.

● The biggest known meteorite weighed 60 tons. It fell in prehistoric times in Namibia, Africa, where it still lies.

● The most famous meteorite crater on Earth is in Arizona. It is nearly a mile wide.

● Not all meteorites are so large. In May 1991 a meteorite weighing over a pound (0.5 kg) fell into a garden in southern England. Some meteors fall as dust.

The giant planets

The giant planets, **Jupiter** and **Saturn**, are the largest planets in the Solar System. Their surfaces are not solid and rocky but are made up of a mixture of turbulent, swirling **gas** and **ice**.

Jupiter

Jupiter, the biggest planet, is so huge that all the other planets in the Solar System could fit inside it.

Saturn

Saturn is smaller than Jupiter, but is very large. It is surrounded by brightly shining rings.

Jupiter facts

● Its day is only 9 hours 50 minutes long (the time it takes to spin around once).

● Its year is 11.9 Earth years long (the time it takes to circle around the Sun).

● Its diameter (through the Equator) is about 88,700 miles (142,800 km).

● There is a very faint ring around it, made of rocky particles. The ring is too faint to be seen from Earth.

● Its atmosphere is made of hydrogen and helium.

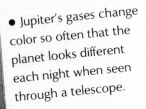

Strange but true

● Jupiter's gases change color so often that the planet looks different each night when seen through a telescope.

● Until the Voyager 1 space probe passed it in 1979, astronomers did not know Jupiter had a ring around it.

● Winds on Saturn blow at about 900 mph (1,400 km/h). Tornadoes on Earth blow at only 180–400 mph (300–600 km/h).

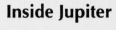

Inside Jupiter

Jupiter is made mainly of **hydrogen**. Its four major layers are:

● A very small rocky core

● An inner layer of hydrogen

● A shell of liquid hydrogen and helium

● A swirling surface of icy clouds

The Great Red Spot

Jupiter's **Great Red Spot** is a swirling **tornado** that has been raging for at least 100 years. It is about 25,000 miles (40,000 km) long and 7,000 miles (11,000 km) wide. That is more than three times the diameter of Earth!

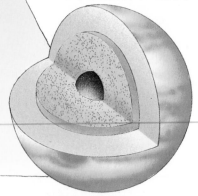

Saturn's rings

Saturn's **rings** are **bands of ice** and **rock** whirling around the planet. The largest rocks are several yards across.

● There are three main rings containing thousands of separate ringlets.

● Saturn's rings are huge but very thin. A sheet of paper 12 feet across would give you a scale model of their depth (the thickness of the paper) compared to their width (the width of the paper).

Voyager space probe

● Voyager probes photographed Saturn's rings and found new satellites

Saturn facts

● Its day (the time it takes to spin around once) is only 10 hours 14 minutes long.

● Its year (the time it takes to circle around the Sun) is 29.5 Earth years.

● Its diameter (across the Equator) is about 75,000 miles (120,000 km).

● Its diameter measured from one side of the ring system to the other is 169,000 miles (272,000 km).

● Its atmosphere is made of hydrogen and helium.

● A bright white area appeared on the surface in September 1990. It is as large as Jupiter's Great Red Spot.

The satellites

Jupiter and Saturn have natural **satellites**, or **moons**, orbiting them. Jupiter has at least 16 moons and Saturn at least 18.

Jupiter's main satellites

● Callisto, the outermost, is an icy and cratered satellite much bigger than Earth's Moon.

● Ganymede is larger than the planet Mercury. Its surface is icy, with grooves and streaks.

● Europa is smaller than Earth's Moon. It is smooth and icy with very few craters.

● Io, the innermost, is slightly larger than the Moon. It has a red, volcanic surface.

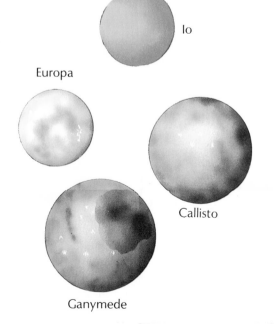

Io

Europa

Callisto

Ganymede

Some of Saturn's satellites

● Mimas (pictured below) is one of the innermost satellites. It has a crater on its surface over 60 miles (100 km) wide. That is nearly two-thirds of its diameter!

● Titan, the largest satellite, is bigger than Mercury. It has a cloudy atmosphere of nitrogen gas, and may have oceans made of liquid methane.

Uranus, Neptune, and Pluto

Uranus, Neptune, and Pluto are the **farthest planets** from the Sun. They are all icy cold. Uranus and Neptune are quite similar to each other and look greenish in color from Earth. Pluto, the tiniest of all the planets, is a dim speck.

In 1985 and 1989, the space probe **Voyager 2** flew past Uranus and Neptune. It took spectacular pictures of the planets, showing details never seen before. It also showed the **rings** around both planets, and discovered an amazing number of new **satellites** — ten for Uranus and six for Neptune.

Uranus

Uranus was discovered in 1781 by **William Herschel**, an amateur astronomer, using a homemade telescope. At first he thought he had found a comet.

Uranus

● Uranus is made up mostly of hydrogen and helium. The gas methane is also present in its atmosphere, which makes Uranus look green from Earth.

Uranus's satellites

Uranus has 15 satellites altogether. The five main ones are Miranda, Ariel, Umbriel, Titania, and Oberon. The largest, Oberon and Titania, are about 900 miles (1,500 km) across.

Umbriel   Oberon
Ariel
Miranda   Titania

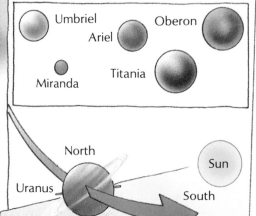

North
Sun
Uranus
South

● Uranus spins on its side instead of almost upright, like the other planets. Because of this, the poles of the planet can sometimes face the Sun. When this happens, they are warmer than the Earth's equator!

● The diameter of Uranus is 32,300 miles (52,000 km). Its day is about 17 hours long, and it takes 84 years to travel around the Sun.

Herschel's telescope

● Until 1986, only nine rings had been counted around Uranus. On its fly-past, however, Voyager 2 found four more rings, making 13 in all.

Strange but true

● Uranus's small satellite, Miranda, may have been shattered in a collision with another body. It seems to have broken up into large pieces which collected together again.

● The cycle of seasons on Triton, Neptune's largest satellite, takes 680 years.

● During the 1990s, Pluto is the nearest it can get to Earth, so it is a very good time to study it. This will not happen again until the 23rd century!

Uranus
1,780 million miles
(2,870 million km)

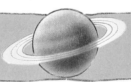
Neptune
2,800 million miles
(4,500 million km)

Pluto
3,660 million miles
(5,900 million km)

Neptune

Neptune was discovered in 1846. It cannot be seen with the naked eye. Through a telescope it looks like a faint blue-green star. Like Uranus, it is surrounded by **rings**.

● Neptune is colder than Uranus. It is about −360°F (−220°C).

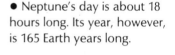
Triton

● Neptune is slightly smaller than Uranus, measuring 30,000 miles (48,400 km) across.

Neptune

● Neptune's day is about 18 hours long. Its year, however, is 165 Earth years long.

Neptune's satellites

Neptune has **eight satellites**. The two main ones are called Triton and Nereid. Triton, the larger, is smaller than Earth's Moon. Very unusually it orbits Neptune in the opposite direction from the planet's own spin.

Nereid

Pluto

Pluto is the **smallest planet**. Because of its orbit (see below) it is usually the farthest away from the Sun. It was not discovered until 1930 and is very difficult to see, even with a telescope.

● Pluto's diameter is 1,800 miles (3,000 km) which means it is smaller than the Moon.

● Pluto's day lasts for just over six Earth days, and its year lasts 248 Earth years.

Pluto

Charon

Pluto's satellite

Pluto has **one known satellite**, Charon. It is 500 miles (800 km) across and is the only satellite apart from Earth's Moon that is not dwarfed by its planet.

Pluto

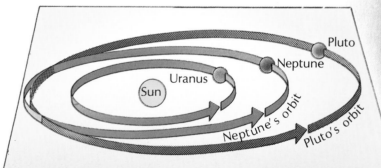

Sun — Uranus — Neptune — Pluto

Neptune's orbit

Pluto's orbit

● Pluto is usually the farthest planet from the Sun. However, its orbit sometimes takes it inside Neptune's orbit. This is happening now, so from 1979 until 1999 Neptune is the "outermost planet."

Planet X?

Astronomers used to think that Uranus and Neptune "wandered" in their orbits because they were pulled by the **gravity** of an unknown space body. They thought there might be another planet — **Planet X** — beyond Pluto. However, this now seems unlikely.

Ancient astronomy

From early times, people have been interested in the stars and planets. They have tried to understand space and how it affects human life. Great **stone circles**, such as Stonehenge in England (built about 3,500 years ago) may have been used to study how the Sun and Moon moved through the sky.

More than 2,000 years ago, the **Chinese**, **Egyptians**, **Babylonians**, and **Greeks** were all skilled astronomers.

The Babylonians

About 3,000 years ago, the **Babylonians** (who used to live in what is now Iraq) studied the stars. They invented **astrology** — the belief that people's lives are influenced by the position of the stars and planets.

● This Babylonian boundary stone shows the importance of the Sun, Moon, and planets to their civilization.

● The Babylonians invented the twelve signs of the zodiac that are still used in astrology.

The Ancient Greeks

The **Greeks** were fine astronomers and mathematicians. In about 240 B.C., Eratosthenes, a Greek mathematician, accurately worked out the **size of the Earth**.

● Here are four of the star groups or constellations (see pp.8–9) named by the Greeks:

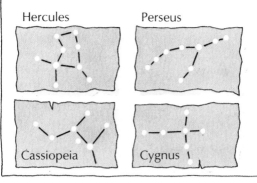

Hercules   Perseus

Cassiopeia   Cygnus

Pioneers of astronomy

Many ancient astronomers added a great deal to our understanding of space. Some were **persecuted** for their discoveries because they went against the teachings of the Christian Church.

● Ptolemy of Alexandria was born in A.D. 120. He believed the Earth was at the center of the Solar System and that the Sun, Moon, and planets circled around it.

● Ptolemy's idea of the Solar System was accepted for 1,300 years.

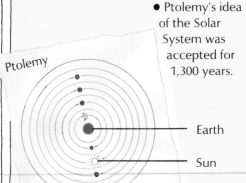

Ptolemy

Earth

Sun

● Nicolaus Copernicus (1473–1543) was a Polish astronomer and mathematician. He published a book that said the Sun, not Earth, was the center of the Solar System. His book was officially banned until 1835.

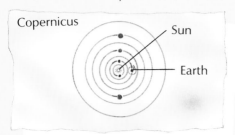

Copernicus

Sun

Earth

● Tycho Brahe (1546–1601) was a Danish astronomer. He wrongly placed Earth back in the center of the Solar System but accurately observed and measured stars, planets and comets.

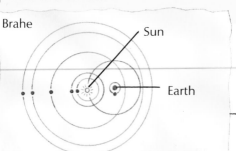

Brahe

Sun

Earth

Early equipment

Before the **telescope** was invented, all astronomy was done with the **naked eye**. However, there were some **instruments** to help astronomers when they studied the sky.

- Ancient Greek sailors studied the stars and the Sun to help them navigate.

- Ancient people knew only five planets: Mercury, Venus, Mars, Jupiter, and Saturn.

- Quadrants and sextants were instruments that enabled astronomers to work out the position of stars and planets.

A modern sextant

An astronomer working out a star's position in the sky by reading the degrees marked on a quadrant.

- Observatories were built to study the sky. This stone-built observatory in India was designed to help people measure the movements of stars and planets and foretell eclipses.

- Johannes Kepler (1571–1630), a German mathematician, put the Sun back in the center of things. He drew up three laws of planetary motion, which are still used today.

Ellipse—

- Kepler correctly showed that a planet's orbit is an ellipse (a squashed circle) rather than a true circle.

- Galileo Galilei (1564–1642) an Italian mathematician, was persecuted for saying that the Sun, not Earth, is the center of the Solar System. He made many discoveries, such as sunspots and Jupiter's four large satellites.

- In 1609, Galileo made one of the first drawings of the Moon's surface.

Galileo's drawing

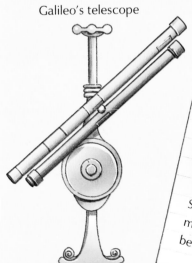

- Galileo was one of the first to use a telescope. This is one of his instruments, which he built soon after telescopes were invented at the beginning of the seventeenth century. He even made the lenses himself. The most powerful of his telescopes magnified, or enlarged, an object thirty times.

Galileo's telescope

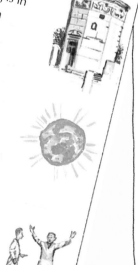

Strange but true

- The oldest observatory building still standing is in Greece. It was built in about 100 B.C..

- Anazagoras, an early Greek philosopher, was banished for saying the Sun was a red-hot stone.

- In 280 B.C. the Greek astronomer Aristarchus said the Sun, not Earth, was the center of the Solar System. It was more than 1,800 years before he was proved right.

Modern Astronomy

The invention of the telescope made it possible to see objects in space more clearly. But the Earth's atmosphere makes them appear blurred and blocks out some important radiation coming from stars and galaxies.

Now there are space telescopes that, outside the haze of Earth's atmosphere, can "see" much more clearly than Earth-based telescopes. They have instruments for detecting X rays and other invisible radiations. They can tell astronomers more about such things as galaxies and black holes.

Telescopes

Telescopes make distant things seem nearer. Light from a distant object enters the tube and the image of the object is then **magnified** (made larger). There are two main kinds of telescope: reflector and refractor.

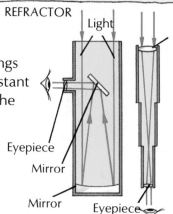

REFRACTOR | Light | REFLECTOR | Lens
Eyepiece | Mirror | Mirror | Eyepiece

- Reflectors: Light is bounced off mirrors into an eyepiece.

- Refractors: Light is focused by lenses.

- Both types of telescope produce upside-down images.

Binoculars

Binoculars are good for giving a **wide, general view** of the night sky, and for tracking moving objects such as satellites.

- Binoculars make distant things look closer but do not magnify as powerfully as telescopes.

Earth-based astronomy

There are many powerful **telescopes on Earth** that provide a good view of space.

- Large optical telescopes produce images that can be analyzed by computer. They are put in buildings on high ground so they can avoid the lights and polluted air of towns and cities.

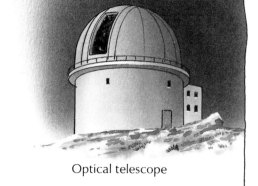

Optical telescope

Radio telescope

- Radio telescopes pick up radio waves from space that are usually produced by clouds of gas or dust. Radio waves are one of the few kinds of space radiation that can pass through Earth's atmosphere.

Kitt Peak observatory

- There are several telescopes on Kitt Peak in Arizona, including a reflector 13 feet (4 m) across. It also has the world's largest solar telescope (for observing the Sun).

- The MMT (Multiple Mirror Telescope) on Mount Hopkins, Arizona, has six mirrors, all 6 ft. (1.8 m) wide. They are positioned by laser beams.

- The largest single radio telescope dish in the world is at Arecibo in Puerto Rico. It is 1,000 ft. (305 m) across.

Arecibo

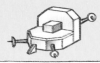
Space telescopes

Space telescopes revolutionized astronomy. They can now be launched by **Space Shuttle** and other craft.

Space telescopes have monitored the **Sun** and invisible **radiation**. They have also observed **stars** and **galaxies**, that could never be studied before.

The Hubble telescope

The Hubble space telescope was launched by the United States on April 24, 1990. It can detect **ultraviolet** and **infrared waves** (see p.7) as well as **visible light**.

(see p.7)

● If all had gone well, Hubble would have transmitted pictures of distant objects never seen before, and stunningly clear images of closer objects.

Space Shuttle

● Unfortunately, Hubble does not work properly. One of its two mirrors is 0.00008 inch (0.0002 cm) too flat — enough to make all its images out of focus.

Telescope

● The fault happened because the equipment used to test the mirror was out of adjustment by just one millimeter.

Solar Panels

The Hubble space telescope

● Despite problems, some pictures have been successful. Pluto and its satellite, Charon, for instance, were seen clearly for the first time.

● The Hubble telescope had other problems after the launch. The telescope wobbles twice for several minutes in each orbit.

● Scientists hope to send astronauts to mend the Hubble telescope. Three similar space telescopes are planned for the future.

Strange but true

● The satellite IRAS discovered the closest known comet to pass Earth for 200 years.

● The radio telescope at Arecibo, Puerto Rico, can pick up signals from up to 15 billion light-years away.

● An astronomer called James Lick, who died in 1876, is buried in the base of the telescope at the Lick Observatory in California.

The Space Age

The Space Age began on October 4, 1957, when Russia launched the satellite **Sputnik 1**. This was a small metal sphere with four thin antennae. It contained a radio transmitter.

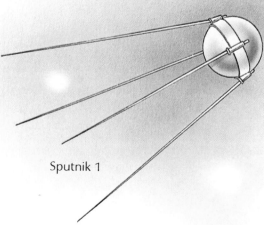

Sputnik 1

During the last thirty years, the development of **spacecraft** has moved incredibly quickly. **Probes**, **satellites**, **rockets**, and **space stations** have been successfully launched and have helped astronomers learn much more about the Solar System and beyond. Satellites also have many other uses for people on Earth (see pp.36–37).

Getting off the ground

The invention of the **rocket** made Space exploration possible.

- As early as 1903, a Russian teacher called Tsiolkovskii suggested using liquid fuel for rockets and proposed rocket-building in separate parts, called stages.

V2

- Weapons called V2 rockets were developed by a German research team and used near the end of World War II. Space rockets were developed from them.

Vostock 1

Laika

- The Russians sent a small dog, called Laika, into orbit in Sputnik 2 in November 1957. She orbited Earth for a week and became the first living thing in space.

- In 1961, Yuri Gagarin, a Soviet cosmonaut, became the first person in space. He orbited Earth once in the spacecraft Vostock 1, landing safely after a 108-minute flight.

Space Shuttle

In 1981, the first **Space Shuttle**, *Columbia*, was launched in the U.S.A. For the first time a spacecraft could go into space and return to Earth, landing like a plane. It could then be used again for another flight.

1. The Shuttle plane, called an orbiter, is launched attached to a giant fuel tank and two solid-fuel boosters.

Orbiter

Boosters

Fuel tank

2. The boosters drop off at a height of 27 miles (43 km). They drop into the sea and are rescued for reuse.

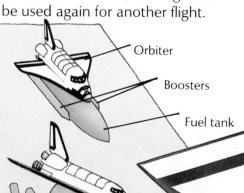

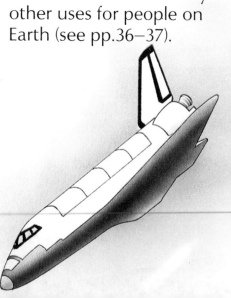

3. At 71 miles (115 km) high, the fuel tank separates and burns up as it falls through Earth's atmosphere. It is the only part of the Shuttle that is not reused.

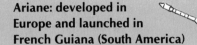

Ariane: developed in Europe and launched in French Guiana (South America)

D-1: the Soviet rocket that launched the Salyut and Mir space stations

Energiya: launcher for the proposed Soviet version of the Space Shuttle

How do rockets work?

Rockets need a great deal of **power** to escape from Earth's gravity. Most have from two to four fuel-burning parts, called **stages**, that lift the rocket into orbit. The stages separate from the rocket as their fuel runs out. Then they burn up in the Earth's atmosphere.

Liquid fuel

Propellant

1. Liquid-fuel rockets work by burning a mixture of fuel and a propellant.

2. The propellant makes the fuel catch fire with an explosive blast that pushes the rocket upward.

3. The rocket then builds up enormous speed — about three times faster than Concorde.

An Apollo Saturn V rocket, like the one used to take people to the Moon (see pp.34–35).

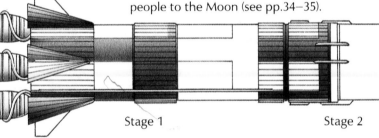

Stage 1

Stage 2

Stage 3

Capsule

Stage 1 separated from the rocket at a height of about 38 miles (61 km).

Stage 2 took the rocket up to about 114 miles (183 km).

Stage 3 took the Apollo capsule into Earth orbit and then to the Moon.

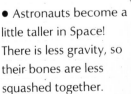

4. The Space Shuttle carries a large cargo. Once in space, the astronauts can repair or rescue satellites, launch new ones, or carry out experiments.

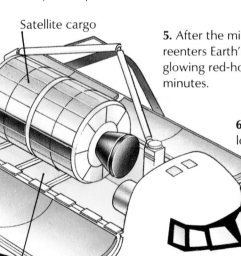

Satellite cargo

Payload bay

5. After the mission, the Shuttle reenters Earth's atmosphere, glowing red-hot for about 10 minutes.

6. It glides down to Earth and lands on a long runway, like an ordinary airplane.

● In 1986, the Space Shuttle *Challenger* exploded 73 seconds after blast-off. All seven astronauts were killed. It happened because of a tiny fault in one of the solid-fuel boosters.

Strange but true

● Yuri Gagarin survived the first manned spaceflight but was killed in a plane crash seven years later.

● Astronauts become a little taller in Space! There is less gravity, so their bones are less squashed together.

● As it comes back into Earth's atmosphere, the Space Shuttle reaches a temperature of 2,300°F (1,260°C).

33

Landing on the Moon

This is some of the equipment used for experiments on the Moon:

Solar wind spectrometer measured the effect of solar wind

The Moon is the only place in the universe that people have **visited**. The effects of the journey on the astronauts, along with their experiments and rock samples, taught scientists a great deal about the Moon.

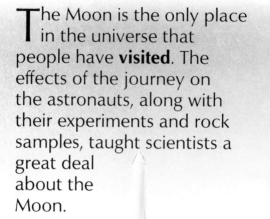

The **first Moon mission**, *Apollo II*, blasted off on July 16, 1969. The enormous Saturn 5 rocket carried the three American astronauts into space with the power of 160 jumbo jets. Four days later, Neil Armstrong stepped onto the Moon's surface and said the famous words: "That's one small step for a man, one giant leap for mankind."

The first Moon landing

Stacked at the top of the **Saturn 5 rocket** were the **Command Module**, the **Service Module**, and the **Lunar module**. Once in orbit around the Moon, the Lunar Module separated to start its journey to the Moon's surface.

- One astronaut, Michael Collins, stayed behind in the Command Module. Neil Armstrong and Edwin Aldrin were in the cramped Lunar Module.

Lunar module

Command module

Service module

The rocket as it was at takeoff.

The Lunar Module coming down to land on the Moon

- Minutes away from landing, Neil Armstrong took the controls, as the automatic navigation was taking them toward rocky ground. They landed safely on the Sea of Tranquillity.

Other Apollo missions

There were six **Apollo missions** between 1969 and 1972. Each one lasted longer than the last, and 842 pounds (382 kg) of Moon rock were collected for analysis.

- On the last three missions, the astronauts used a Moon buggy called the Lunar Rover.

The Soviet missions

- In 1959, the Soviet unmanned probe, Luna 1, flew close to the Moon. A few months later Luna 2 landed on the Moon's surface. It was the first Earth-made object to land on another world.

- Soon after, Luna 3 flew past the far side of the Moon and took the first pictures of it.

- In 1966, Luna 9 landed on the Moon's surface and took the first close-up pictures of it.

Luna 9

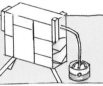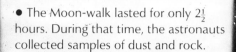

- The Moon-walk lasted for only 2½ hours. During that time, the astronauts collected samples of dust and rock.

- They also put up a U.S. flag, which they had to stiffen with wire as there is no wind on the Moon to blow it!

- The Moon has six times less gravity than Earth. This means that on the Moon astronauts weigh only a sixth of their normal weight. They could jump and spring about with ease, but it was difficult to walk.

- The astronauts tried to sleep in the Lunar Module but it was much too cold. At night, temperatures on the Moon reach −240°F (−150°C).

- The astronauts had to use special tools to collect rock samples, because they could not bend over in their spacesuits.

Moon discoveries

On Earth the surface is changing all the time. The Moon, however, is a dead place with **no atmosphere** and **no weather** to erode and change the landscape. So Moon dust and rock have lain in the same positions for millions of years. The youngest **Moon rock** analyzed was 3.1 billion years old.

Moon rock

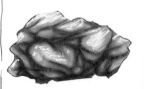

- One sample of Moon rock was found to be about 4.6 billion years old — about the same age as Earth.

Moonquake detector

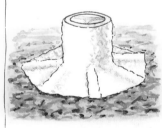

- Instruments detecting "moonquakes" found them to be much weaker than earthquakes.

The Moon

- Because of the Apollo missions, the Moon has now been mapped more accurately than before.

Strange but true

- Astronauts' footprints and Lunar Rover tire tracks will stay on the Moon for millions of years as there is no wind to blow them away.

- The Moon is completely quiet, because there is no air to carry sound.

- Nothing can grow on the Moon, but plants did grow in Moon-soil on Earth.

Satellites

There are about 200 **artificial satellites** whirling around the Earth. There is also lots of junk in space, such as the remains of old satellites. Thousands have been launched and worked for a while before being replaced.

Satellites do all kinds of different jobs. Some can study Earth's **land** and **weather**, or beam **television pictures** and **telephone calls** across the world. Some can analyze **space radiation** that cannot penetrate the Earth's atmosphere. Some are used to **spy** on other countries.

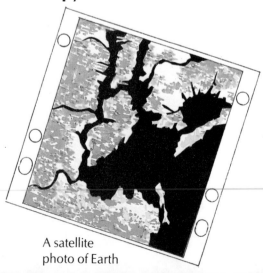

A satellite photo of Earth

Getting into orbit

Satellites are taken into space by **rockets** or by **Space Shuttle**. They are carried in the Shuttle's cargo, or payload, bay and then launched into orbit in Space.

• These are some of the kinds of orbit a satellite might use:

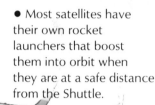

• Sometimes a robot arm, controlled by a Shuttle astronaut, lifts a satellite out of the payload bay and launches it.

• Most satellites have their own rocket launchers that boost them into orbit when they are at a safe distance from the Shuttle.

• Geostationary orbit: the satellite orbits at the same speed as Earth's spin. It is always above the same point on Earth, at a height of about 22,000 miles (36,000 km).

• Polar orbit: the satellite orbits Earth from north to south, and can cover most of the Earth within a day. This orbit is usually at a height of about 620 miles (1,000 km).

• Eccentric orbit: the satellite flies low over parts of the Earth before swinging out to complete the orbit.

Different kinds of satellites

Communications satellites (comsats) beam telephone calls and television pictures from one part of the world to another. They receive a picture from Earth and send it on to its destination.

A Molniya satellite

• In 1965, Russian Molniya satellites began the world's biggest network of comsats.

Intelsat 6

Power from Space

Satellites have large **solar panels** to trap energy from the Sun.

• Satellites store the Sun's energy in batteries and use it to power their equipment.

• Intelsat 6 carries 120,000 telephone circuits and three television channels.

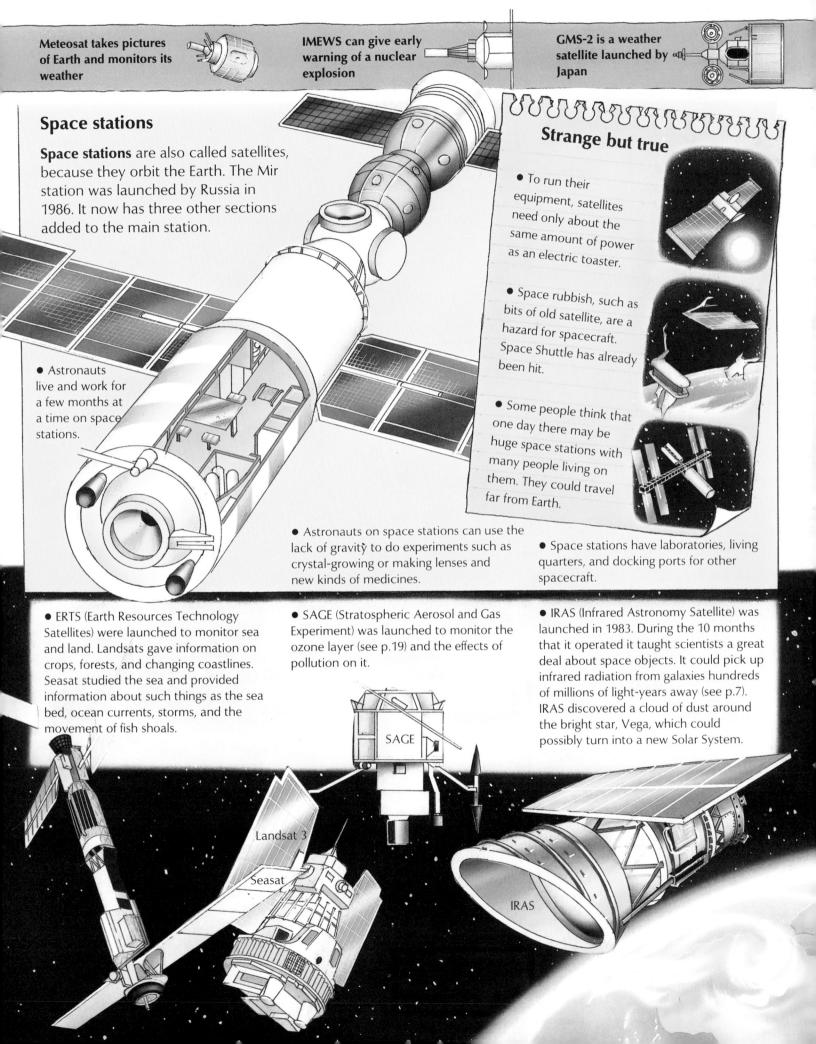

Meteosat takes pictures of Earth and monitors its weather

IMEWS can give early warning of a nuclear explosion

GMS-2 is a weather satellite launched by Japan

Space stations

Space stations are also called satellites, because they orbit the Earth. The Mir station was launched by Russia in 1986. It now has three other sections added to the main station.

- Astronauts live and work for a few months at a time on space stations.

- Astronauts on space stations can use the lack of gravity to do experiments such as crystal-growing or making lenses and new kinds of medicines.

Strange but true

- To run their equipment, satellites need only about the same amount of power as an electric toaster.

- Space rubbish, such as bits of old satellite, are a hazard for spacecraft. Space Shuttle has already been hit.

- Some people think that one day there may be huge space stations with many people living on them. They could travel far from Earth.

- Space stations have laboratories, living quarters, and docking ports for other spacecraft.

- ERTS (Earth Resources Technology Satellites) were launched to monitor sea and land. Landsats gave information on crops, forests, and changing coastlines. Seasat studied the sea and provided information about such things as the sea bed, ocean currents, storms, and the movement of fish shoals.

- SAGE (Stratospheric Aerosol and Gas Experiment) was launched to monitor the ozone layer (see p.19) and the effects of pollution on it.

- IRAS (Infrared Astronomy Satellite) was launched in 1983. During the 10 months that it operated it taught scientists a great deal about space objects. It could pick up infrared radiation from galaxies hundreds of millions of light-years away (see p.7). IRAS discovered a cloud of dust around the bright star, Vega, which could possibly turn into a new Solar System.

SAGE

Landsat 3

Seasat

IRAS

Space probes

Space probes have been some of the most successful developments of the Space Age. They have taught astronomers a great deal about the **Solar System** by visiting all the planets except Pluto. Scientists now have much more information about **planets** and their **satellites**, as well as amazing pictures.

In 1959, the Soviet probe **Luna 1** was the first to by-pass the Moon. Thirty years later, in 1989, **Voyager 2** sent back the first detailed pictures of Neptune. The U.S. probe **Galileo**, launched in 1989, will reach Jupiter in 1995. It will orbit the planet and send a probe into its deadly atmosphere.

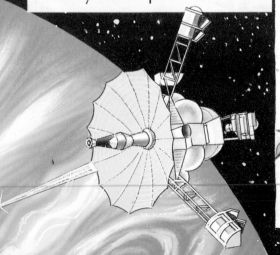

Probes to the nearest planets

In 1974–5 the U.S. probe **Mariner 10** flew past Mercury three times. It took 8,000 pictures, all showing the same side of the planet. These are some probes and their achievements:

- Mariner's pictures of Mercury show it to be covered in craters.

- Mariner also flew past Venus and took dramatic pictures of its swirling clouds.

Mariner

- Soviet Venera probes 9 and 10 landed on Venus and sent back photographs.

Viking

- In 1976, two Viking probes landed on Mars, studied the climate and tested the soil for signs of life. They found none.

- More Mars probes are planned. They may lead to people landing on Mars within the next 50 years.

Pioneer probes

- Pioneers 10 and 11 were the first probes to brave the dangers of the Asteroid Belt on their journey to Jupiter and Saturn.

- Giotto found that the comet's solid nucleus was 9 miles (15 km) wide.

- Pioneer 10 flew past Jupiter in 1973, sending information back to Earth by radio signals. It is now farther than Pluto from the Sun.

- The Giotto probe intercepted Halley's comet in 1986. It flew right into the comet's tail. Despite being damaged, it was able to send back information.

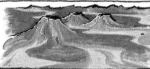
Voyager probes

The two **Voyager** probes, launched in 1977, have given stunning new information about the **outer planets**. Both probes flew past Jupiter and Saturn, and Voyager 2 sent back the first detailed pictures of Uranus, Neptune, and their satellites.

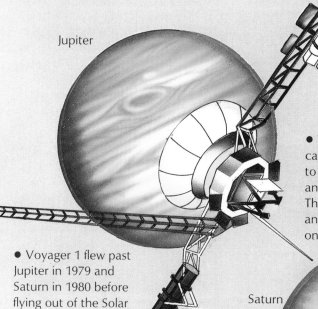

Jupiter

Voyager 1

● Voyager probes carried TV cameras and special equipment to measure such things as heat and magnetic fields on planets. They each had a large radio antenna and carried experiments on a central work ring.

● Voyager 1 flew past Jupiter in 1979 and Saturn in 1980 before flying out of the Solar System.

Saturn

Voyager messages

Both Voyager probes carry **messages** in case they are intercepted by **aliens**. They include:

● Pictures of a man, woman, and child and a map of the Solar System, showing where Earth is.

● A record containing music and greetings in various languages. There are 118 pictures stored on the record, giving a more detailed view of Earth.

Strange but true

● Pioneer and Voyager probes may survive for millions of years, drifting in Space.

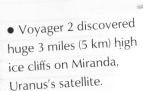

● Voyager 2 discovered huge 3 miles (5 km) high ice cliffs on Miranda, Uranus's satellite.

● If Voyager had existed a few years earlier, it might have been possible to send it to visit Pluto as well, when Pluto was nearer the other outer planets.

● Voyager 2 flew past Jupiter in 1979, Saturn in 1981, Uranus in 1986 and Neptune in 1989. It discovered ten satellites of Uranus and six of Neptune.

● Voyager probes could visit so many planets because between 1979 and 1989 the planets farthest from the Sun were lined up together. This happens only once every 175 years.

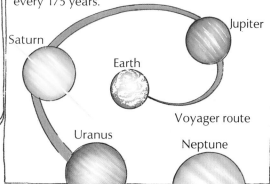

Jupiter

Saturn

Earth

Voyager route

Uranus

Neptune

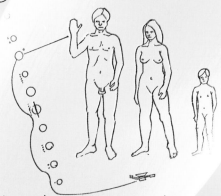

Uranus

Neptune

● Voyager photographed Neptune's Great Dark Spot — a storm similar to Jupiter's Great Red Spot (see p.24).

The Future

Space exploration is hugely expensive. Nevertheless, plans are underway for large orbiting **space stations** and **permanent bases** on the Moon and Mars. Eventually, people may live on a planet other than Earth. It might even be possible to travel to other stars and set up bases in their Solar Systems.

Materials from outside Earth would be used to build bases on nearby planets. Rocks from the Moon and asteroids, for example, could be used for building materials. Astronauts would be sent to work on these projects.

Moon base

A Moon base could become a reality in the fairly near future, with astronauts living and working there for long periods.

Mars base

Within the next 50 years or so, people may have walked on Mars. They may even have started building the first **Mars base**.

The cost of space exploration

How much new space exploration takes place will depend on whether governments can afford the **cost**:

● From 1961–72, the U.S.A. spent about 25.5 billion dollars on getting astronauts to the Moon.

● From 1958–73, the U.S.S.R. spent about 45 billion dollars on its space program.

● At first, an observatory with powerful radio telescopes may be set up on the far side of the Moon. This would enable deep space to be studied, away from radio interference from Earth. People at the observatory could also study the Moon and do experiments.

● Eventually, a permanent base could be set up on the Moon. The main industry would be mining Moon rock.

● A Moon base could help scientists plan manned landings on Mars. This is why the Moon was called a "bridge between two worlds" by the U.S. National Commission on Space.

● A base on Mars would be slow to build. It would take many missions, and many years, for astronauts to complete the work. They would have to spend eight months traveling in space before they reached the planet.

● Some scientists believe that it may be better to set up a base on Phobos, Mars's larger satellite. Because of Phobos's weak gravity, it would be easier for spacecraft to approach and land there.

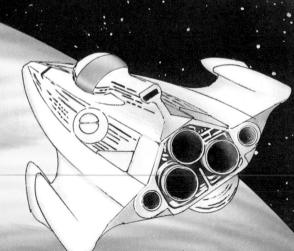

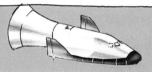
Near-future spaceflight

The U.S.A., Britain, Japan, and Germany all have plans for a new hypersonic **aerospace plane**. It would take off rather like a jet fighter, burning **oxygen** from the atmosphere rather than oxidizer (see p.33). Rockets would then fire to take it into orbit.

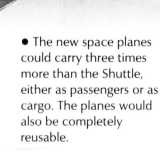

● The new space planes could carry three times more than the Shuttle, either as passengers or as cargo. The planes would also be completely reusable.

Power from Space

New sources of power for people on Earth could be found in space. **Space power stations** would be built to do this.

● A gigantic solar panel could be sent into orbit to capture the Sun's energy and beam it back to Earth.

An artist's impression of what the space power station might look like

● The power station would probably have to be built in space.

● One idea is to set up a "factory" in a low orbit. Completed parts would then be moved into a higher orbit and used to build the station, which would orbit above one place on Earth.

Freedom space station

The U.S.A. hopes to launch the first part of its planned **Freedom space station** in 1995. It will be the biggest-ever space station, and the first permanent one.

● The Space Shuttle will take parts of the station into orbit over the course of 20 missions.

● Much research could be done on the station, ranging from monitoring the long-term effects on people of living in space, to growing near-perfect crystals in the low gravity.

● Astronauts will assemble the station in space.

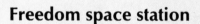

● Russia designed a new space station, Mir 2, to be launched in 1994, but has had to cancel it because of the cost.

Strange but true

● One idea for a space power station includes an orbiting solar panel that would be 13 miles (21 km) long and 3 miles (5 km) wide!

● In 1865 the French writer Jules Verne wrote a story about people traveling to the Moon from a launch site in Florida. A hundred years later, Apollo astronauts did exactly that!

● There could be millions of inhabited planets like Earth. Nobody knows what the inhabitants might look like!

Space facts and lists

Stars

- About 1,500 stars are visible at night with the naked eye in a clear, dark, sky.

- There are 88 constellations altogether.

- The smallest known star measures about 1,000 miles (1,700 km) across. It is a white dwarf called LP 327–16.

Supernovae

Supernovae are exploding stars. Here are four recorded supernovae explosions seen with the naked eye. The first one was recorded by the Chinese, who said that the supernova was visible for two years.

Date	Constellation	Brightness
1006	Lupus (Wolf)	−9.5 (very bright)
1054	Taurus (Bull)	−4
1572	Cassiopeia	−4
1604	Ophiuchus (Serpent-Bearer)	−3

- At its brightest, a supernova can be 500 million times as bright as the Sun.

- There was a supernova in 1987 in the Large Magellanic Cloud — our closest galaxy.

- A cloud of dust and gas called the Crab Nebula is the remains of the supernova seen in 1054.

Galaxies

These are the nearest galaxies to the Milky Way.

Name	Distance	Diameter
	(Light-years)	
Large Magellanic Cloud	180,000	30,000
Small Magellanic Cloud	190,000	16,000
Ursa Minor dwarf	250,000	2,000
Draco dwarf	250,000	3,000
Sextant dwarf	280,000	6,000
Sculptor dwarf	280,000	5,000
Fornax dwarf	420,000	7,000
Carina dwarf	550,000	3,000
Leo I	750,000	2,000

Solar eclipses

- The longest total eclipse of the Sun recorded was on June 20, 1955. It lasted for 7 minutes, 8 seconds.

- The first recorded eclipse of the Sun was in China on October 22, 2136 B.C.

- There are usually two to four solar eclipses each year. However, occasionally there are five. This last happened in 1935.

Here are the dates of the eclipses of the Sun between 1992–2000.

Year	Visible in	Kind of eclipse
1992		
4/5 January	Central Pacific	Annular
30 June	S. Atlantic	Total
24 December	Arctic	Partial
1993		
21 May	Arctic	Partial
13 November	Antarctic·	Partial
1994		
10 May	Pacific, Mexico U.S.A., Canada	Annular
3 November	Peru, Brazil S. Atlantic	Total
1995		
29 April	S. Pacific, Brazil Peru, S. Atlantic	Annular
24 October	Iran, India, E. Indies, Pacific	Total

Year	Visible in	Kind of eclipse
1996		
17 April	Antarctic	Partial
12 October	Arctic	Partial
1997		
9 March	Russia, Arctic	Total
2 September	Antarctic	Partial
1998		
26 February	Pacific, South of Panama, Atlantic	Total
22 August	Indian Ocean E. Indies, Pacific	Annular
1999		
16 February	Indian Ocean Australia, Pacific	Annular
11 August	Atlantic, England, France, Turkey, India	Total

- An annular eclipse happens when the Moon is too far away to cover the Sun completely. A ring of light appears around the Moon.

The Moon

- The biggest "sea" on the Moon is the Mare Imbrium (Sea of Showers), which is 800 miles (1,300 km) across.

- The biggest Moon crater visible from Earth is Bailly, which is 183 miles (295 km) wide and $2\frac{1}{2}$ miles (4 km) deep.

- The deepest Moon crater is Newton, which is over 5 miles (8 km) deep.

- There are about 1,500 moonquakes a year. They are usually 400–700 miles (700–1,100 km) below the surface and are much weaker than earthquakes.

Lunar eclipses

These are the dates of Lunar eclipses between 1992 and 2000.

Date	Type	Mid-point of eclipse
1992		
15 June	Partial	4.58 am
9 December	Total	11.45 pm
1993		
4 June	Total	1.02 pm
29 November	Total	6.26 am
1994		
25 May	Partial	3.32 am
1995		
15 April	Partial	12.19 pm
1996		
4 April	Total	12.11 am
27 September	Total	2.55 am
1997		
24 March	Partial	4.41 am
16 September	Total	6.47 pm
1999		
28 July	Partial	11.34 am
2000		
21 January	Total	4.45 am
16 July	Total	1.57 pm

Comets

● Halley's Comet is the brightest comet seen regularly. It passes the Sun every 76.1 years.

● People used to believe that a comet's appearance signaled an important event about to happen on Earth.

● Comet West, which was visible in daylight in 1976, may take a million years to orbit the Sun.

● The comet with the shortest orbit is Encke's. It takes 3.3 years to travel around the Sun.

● The biggest comet was recorded in 1811. The head was 1.2 million miles (2 million km) in diameter and the tail was 100 million miles (160 million km) long.

● The Great Comet of 1843 had the longest recorded tail — 205 million miles (330 million km).

These are some comets that have been observed more than once:

Name	Years taken to circle the Sun
Enke	3.3
D'Arrest	6.2
Wolf-Harrington	6.6
Shajn-Schaldach	7.3
Smirnova-Chernykh	8.5
Slaughter-Burnham	11.6
Temple-Tuttle	32.9
Pons-Brooks	71
Halley	76.1
Herschel-Rigollet	156

Meteors

● Every year the Earth passes through groups of meteoroids. As Earth passes through them, showers of meteors can be seen in the sky.

● To see meteors, you need patience and a clear night sky, away from city lights, and with no moonlight.

● The most spectacular meteor shower that takes place each year is called the Perseids. They are visible around August 12.

● During the Perseids meteor shower, several dozen meteors can be seen every hour for several hours.

Meteorite craters

These are the names and sizes of some meteorite craters on Earth:

Name	Diameter (feet)
Meteor Crater, Arizona	4,150
Wolf Creek, Australia	2,800
Henbury, Australia	650
Boxhole, Australia	570
Odessa, Texas	550
Waqar, Arabia	330
Desel, Estonia	330
Campo del Cielo, Argentina	250
Dalgaranga, Australia	230
Sikhote-Alin, Siberia	90

These are the weights of some of the biggest meteorites ever found:

Meteorite	Weight
Hoba west, Grootfontein, South Africa	60 tons
Armanty, Outer Mongolia	20 tons
Willamette, Oregon	14 tons
Campo del Cielo, Argentina	13 tons
Mundrabilla, Australia	12 tons
Magura, Czechoslovakia	1.5 tons

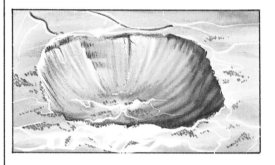

Asteroids

● The biggest asteroid is Ceres, with a diameter of 580 miles (940 km).

● The smallest known asteroid is probably Hathor. Its diameter is about 0.3 mile (0.5 km).

● Vesta is the brightest asteroid. Arethusa is the darkest.

● The asteroid Hermes came within 500,000 miles (800,000 km) of Earth on October 28, 1937.

● An asteroid called the NORC was named after an electronic calculator. Most asteroids are named by their discoverers, who can choose any name they like.

Space facts and lists

Astronomy dates

1543
Copernicus published the book in which he stated that the Sun, not Earth, was the center of the Solar System.

1576–1596
Tycho Brahe drew up the most accurate star catalog ever made without a telescope.

1600
Giordano Bruno was burned at the stake for publicly stating that the Earth goes around the Sun.

1604
Kepler's Star was the last supernova to be seen in our galaxy, to date.

1608
The telescope was invented in Holland by Hans Lippershey.

1668
Isaac Newton made the first reflecting telescope.

1758
Halley's Comet returned, as had been predicted for the first time.

1781
The astronomer William Herschel discovered Uranus.

1801
Ceres was the first asteroid to be discovered.

1846
Neptune was discovered, using the predictions of its position made by John Adams and Urbain Leverrier.

1850
The first successful photograph of a star (Vega) was produced.

1908
There was a mysterious explosion in Tunguska, Siberia, which was thought to be caused by a meteorite landing.

1930
Astronomer Clyde Tombaugh discovered Pluto.

1937
The first radio telescope dish was built. It measured 30 ft. (9.4 m) across.

1963
Quasars were identified for the first time.

1967
Pulsars were discovered.

1986
Halley's Comet returned as predicted. The probe *Giotto* passed through the comet's tail and sent back information about the comet's head.

1990
The Hubble space telescope was launched.

Space Age firsts

● The first object to orbit Earth was *Sputnik 1*, launched by Russia in October 1957.

● The first animal in Space was the Soviet dog, Laika, in November 1957. It died on the flight.

● The first animals to survive an orbital spaceflight were the Soviet dogs, Strelka and Belka, launched in *Sputnik 5* in August 1960.

● The first person to orbit Earth was Yuri Gagarin, from Russia, in April 1961.

● The first American to orbit Earth was John Glenn in February 1962.

● The first woman in space was Valentina Tereshkova, from Russia, in June 1963.

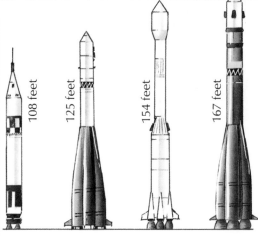

Some space rockets and their heights

Titan   Vostock   Ariane   Soyuz

108 feet   125 feet   154 feet   167 feet

● The first docking in space of two manned spacecraft was in January 1969. The spacecraft were the Soviet *Soyuz 4* and *5*. Two cosmonauts spacewalked to *Soyuz 4*.

● The first person to walk on the Moon was Neil Armstrong in July 1969.

● The first vehicle on the Moon was the unmanned Soviet Lunokhod Rover in November 1970.

● The first landing on Venus was by the Soviet *Venera 3* probe in March 1966.

● The first space station to be launched was the Soviet *Salyut 1* in April 1971.

● The first space probe sent to the outer planets, was *Pioneer 10*, launched in March 1972. It passed out of the Solar System after its mission.

● The first U.S. space station, *Skylab 1*, was launched in May 1973.

● The first Space Shuttle, *Columbia*, was sent into orbit by the United States in April 1981.

● The first U.S. woman in space was Sally Ride in 1983.

● The first astronaut to fly untethered in space, using a self-propelling backpack called a Manned Maneuvering Unit (MMU), was American Bruce McCandless in February 1984.

● The first British person in space was Helen Sharman in May 1991.

Rocket launch centers

Here are the world's main rocket launch centers:

U.S.A.:
   Cape Canaveral, Florida
   Vandenberg Air Force Base, California
   Wallops Station, Virginia
RUSSIA:
   Baikonu Cosmodrome
   Plesetsk
   Kapustin Yar
JAPAN:
   Kagoshima Space Center
   Tanegashima, Osaki
CHINA:
   Jiuquan Satellite Launch Center
   Xi Chang Satellite Launch Center
   Taiyuan Satellite Launch Center
ESA (European Space Agency):
   Guiana Space Center, Kourou, French
     Guiana
ITALY:
   San Marco Launch Platform, Formosa
     Bay, Kenya
INDIA:
   Sriharikota Launching Range (SHAR)
ISRAEL:
   Palmachim Air Force Base

Giant telescopes

These are the biggest telescopes in the world:

Reflectors

Name	Aperture
Keck Telescope, Hawaii	982 cm
Mount Semirodriki, Russia	600 cm
Palomar, California	508 cm
Mount Hopking, California	440 cm
La Palma, Canary Islands	420 cm
Cerro Tololo, Chile	401 cm
Kitt Peak, Arizona	401 cm
Siding Spring, Australia	389 cm

Refractors

Yerkes, Williams Bay	102 cm
Lick, California	91 cm
Meudon, France	83 cm
Potsdam, Germany	81 cm
Alleghany, Pittsburgh	76 cm
Nice, France	76 cm

Radio Telescopes

● The biggest non-steerable radio dish is in Arecibo, Puerto Rico. It measures 1,000 ft. (305 m) across.

● The biggest steerable radio dish is in the Max Planck Institute, Bonn, Germany. It is 330 ft. (100 m).

● The biggest group, or array, of radio antennae is in New Mexico. There are 27 antennae, all 82 ft. (25 m) wide. The array is Y-shaped and each arm measures 69 ft. (21 m).

Manned Moon missions

All manned missions to the Moon to date were made by U.S. astronauts in Apollo spacecraft during the late 1960s and early 1970s.

Date	Mission	Astronauts
July 1969	Apollo 11	Neil Armstrong Edwin Aldrin Michael Collins
Nov 1969	Apollo 12	Charles Conrad Richard Gordon Alan Bean
April 1970	Apollo 13 (abandoned)	James Lovell John Swigert Fred Haise
Feb 1971	Apollo 14	Alan Shepard Stuart Roosa Edgar Mitchell
July 1971	Apollo 15	David Scott James Irwin Alfred Worden
April 1972	Apollo 16	John Young Thomas Mattingly Charles Duke
Dec 1972	Apollo 17	Eugene Cernan Ronald Evans Harrison Schmitt

Space probes

Here are some of the main space probes that have been launched:

1959
Luna 1, 2, and 3 (Russia) became the first successful probes to the Moon.

1965
Mariner 4 (U.S.A.) took pictures of Mars.

1966
Luna 9 (Russia) landed on the Moon.

1967
Venera 4 (Russia) landed on Venus.

1971
Mariner 9 (U.S.A.) was put into orbit around Mars and took photographs of surface.

1976
Vikings 1 and 2 (U.S.A.) landed on Mars.

1978
Veneras 11 and 12 (Russia) and two Pioneer probes (U.S.A.) visited Venus.

1979
Voyager 1 (U.S.A.) by-passed Jupiter.

1980
Voyager 1 (U.S.A.) by-passed Saturn.

1986
Voyager 2 (U.S.A.) by-passed Uranus. Five probes, including Giotto (U.S.A.), were sent to intercept Halley's Comet.

1989
Voyager 2 (U.S.A.) by-passed Neptune. Phobos 2 (Russia) entered orbit around Mars. Galileo (U.S.A.) was launched, eventually bound for Jupiter.

1991
Magellan (U.S.A.) sent back detailed information about Venus after mapping most of its surface by radar.

INDEX